anythink

D0772566

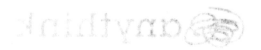

GENIUS COMMUNICATION INVENTIONS

FROM MORSE CODE TO THE INTERNET

Yay! Only 1,285 pages still to print...

Thanks to the creative team:
Senior Editor: Alice Peebles
Fact Checking: Tom Jackson
Design: www.collaborate.agency

Hungry Tomato®
A division of Lerner Publishing Group, Inc.
241 First Avenue North
Minneapolis, MN 55401 USA

For reading levels and more information, look up this title at www.lernerbooks.com.

Main body text set in Josefin Slab SemiBold 10.5/12.
Typeface provided by Font Squirrel.

Library of Congress Cataloging-in-Publication Data

Names: Turner, Matt, 1964- author. | Conner, Sarah, illustrator.
Title: Genius communication inventions : from Morse code to the internet / Matt Turner ; Sarah Conner [illustrator].
Description: Minneapolis : Hungry Tomato, [2018] | Series: Incredible inventions | Audience: Ages 8-12. | Audience: Grades 4 to 6. | Includes index.
Identifiers: LCCN 2016056353 (print) | LCCN 2016059228 (ebook) | ISBN 9781512432107 (lb : alk. paper) | ISBN 9781512450088 (eb pdf)
Subjects: LCSH: Inventions—History—Juvenile literature. | Telecommunication—History—Juvenile literature. | Written communication—History—Juvenile literature. | Computer networks—Juvenile literature.
Classification: LCC T48 .T867 2018 (print) | LCC T48 (ebook) | DDC 609—dc23

LC record available at https://lccn.loc.gov/2016056353

Manufactured in the United States of America
1-41765-23526-3/3/2017

GENIUS COMMUNICATION INVENTIONS

FROM MORSE CODE TO THE INTERNET

by Matt Turner
Illustrated by Sarah Conner

HUNGRY TOMATO®

Minneapolis

German schoolteacher Johann Reis invented a telephone in 1861. To see what the horse is up to, turn to page 18.

CONTENTS

IN TOUCH

The history of communication takes us from the invention of alphabets and writing, the printing press, and the use of electricity in telegraph and telephone right through to our modern digital age with its computers, satellites, and smartphones.

Our earliest ancestors made stunning drawings on cave walls, so maybe they spoke just as beautifully as they sat around the fire at night. We'll never know, though, because we have no record of their languages— alphabets had not yet been written. Even into modern times, some cultures didn't bother with writing. The Maori of New Zealand, for instance, only began writing down words in the 1820s, after Europeans visited them. But their traditional tattoos and carvings are a kind of language in themselves.

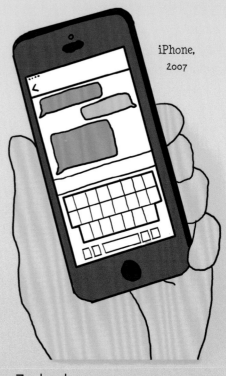

iPhone, 2007

Communicating in the present day is easier and faster than ever, and it takes many forms. In any single day, we might use telephone, email, text, Facebook, Twitter, Skype, Instagram, and more. We sometimes text other family

Paper, 105 CE

members even if they're in the same room! In a peculiar way, we've come full circle back to cave days, speaking directly (electronically) to our friends—even those in other countries—rather than writing them a letter.

Here we look at how those big changes happened. Some were slow, such as the gradual, century-by-century changes to ancient picture alphabets. Others have been quick. The Internet, for instance, is less than fifty years old, and Facebook is still a teenager.

Find out who invented paper and pens, printing, email, and Instagram. And have fun with some hilarious predictions made by stick-in-the-muds who couldn't see any future for radio, television, cinema, computer . . .

First fax machine, 1840

Vacuum tube (in radio), 1904

Video cassette recorder, 1950s

LANGUAGE

Language is as old as humanity itself. Writing originally came from art. If you wanted to say *sun* or *bear*, you drew a picture of the sun or a bear. Over the years, these drawings became coded letter systems: alphabets. Around the world, there are currently more than 6,000 different languages. However, except for the most recent languages, we simply can't say who invented them.

FIRST ALPHABET

People first used alphabets about 5,200 years ago in the Middle East, mainly for writing about taxes and trading. This Sumerian scribe is using a reed to punch wedge shapes in wet clay, which later dried. Sumerian wedge-letter writing is called cuneiform.

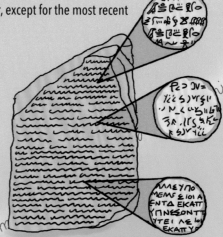

ROSETTA STONE

Ancient Egyptian priests used pictograms we call hieroglyphs (holy carvings). For ages, we didn't know what these meant. But in 1799, a French soldier in Egypt discovered an old stone tablet carrying the same message in three languages. At last we could work out what those priests were scribbling.

Original pictogram	Later pictogram	Assyrian cuneiform	Meaning
			Mountains
			Fish
			Ox
			Grain
			To Go

PICTOGRAMS

The very earliest writers used pictograms—shapes describing things. So, a pictogram for *water* was often a wavy line, and *ox* was a horned head. Later, people began using simpler shapes, which were quicker to draw than pictograms. (Lk txtn ur frnds.) This table shows some early writing systems from the ancient Middle East.

PITMAN SHORTHAND

Fast-forward to 1830s England, where a teacher, Isaac Pitman, believed that people spent too long writing. "Time saved is life gained," he said. Too right! Isaac invented a shorthand language of simple lines and squiggles. Each shape stood for a sound or for a simple word (such as *the* or *you*). Pitman shorthand is still popular, saving people time.

Makes perfect sense to me!

SIGNALS

Before radio, sailors hung flags like laundry on their ships' masts to send signals. Captain Fred Marryat devised a basic flag code in 1817, and forty years later it grew into the International Code of Signals, with twenty-six flags. You can send a message with a single flag: the A flag means "I have a diver down." Or you can string several flags together to make words.

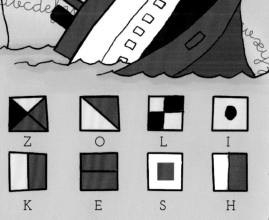

Z O L I

K E S H

Tio estas hundo!

I beg your pardon?

ESPERANTO

Esperanto is a language invented in 1887 by Polish doctor Ludwig Zamenhof. He wanted to make it so easy that anyone could use it, a kind of international language. Currently, more than two million people can speak Esperanto.

WRITING IT DOWN

The material that is written **on** is as important as the writing. You can't carry stone tablets to the shops! Early people made writing material from plant fibers and parchment from animal skins. Paper came much later, and pencils and pens are really very recent.

SYMBOLS

The very earliest writing that has been found is a group of symbols found at Jiahu in China. They were carved onto tortoiseshells and bones about 8,500 years ago. No one's quite sure what the symbols mean. Magic spells, perhaps.

Grandad?

What a pong!

PAPER

The ancient Egyptians mashed strips of papyrus, a marsh plant, into flat sheets for writing on, and so gave us the word paper. Around 105 CE in China, Tsai Lun made wrapping paper from rags, bark, and old nets.

OWW!

INK

For ink, early Chinese used a mixture of boiled animal skin, burnt bones, burnt tar, and soot. Phew, stinky!

TATTOOING

Centuries ago, the Maori of New Zealand made tattoo ink from caterpillars, burnt tree gum, and used sharks' teeth as tattoo tools. When Europeans arrived, Maori began adding gunpowder to their ink.

POST-ITS

The great thing about sticky Post-It notes is that they're not too sticky, so you can reuse them lots of times. American Arthur Fry invented the Post-It note in 1974. He used a not-too-sticky glue invented a few years earlier by Spencer Silver.

I INVENTED THIS!

GRRR!

Don't even think about it!

STAMPS

The first glue-backed stamp was the British Penny Black of 1840. Rowland Hill, a teacher, introduced it to make letters easier and cheaper to send. To buy an original Penny Black today, you'll need $3.8–5 million!

BIROS

The ballpoint pen is sometimes called the "biro" after Hungarian László Biró, its inventor in the 1930s. Or was he? In fact, it was American John Loud's idea in 1888. He used his ballpoint for writing on leather (when no longer on the cow), but he never benefited from his invention.

Better than wearing an ear tag!

MINE

MINE

MINE

PENCILS

The first pencils were simple sticks of graphite dug from mines in the hills of Cumbria in northern England as many as 500 years ago. Shepherds used them to identify their sheep.

PRINTING

The invention of printing was one of the biggest technological leaps in human history. It meant that if you learned to read, you could learn anything written in books. Like these little facts. So it's slightly surprising that printing took so long—more than 1,000 years—to spread from its birthplace in China to the cities of Europe.

WOODBLOCK PRINTING

Chinese Buddhist monks began woodblock printing as early as 200 CE. They carved pictures, such as flowers, and text into wood, then used the carvings to print on silk. Like a rubber stamp, the uncut parts made inky marks. The cutaway parts did not.

DOH!

TYPEWRITER

American William Burt came up with the typographer—possibly the world's first typewriter—in 1829, but it didn't work terribly well. He'd invented it to make secretaries work faster, but it was actually slower than handwriting!

TOY PRINTMAKER

This John Bull Printing Outfit, made by Carson Baker Ltd of London, was a popular toy in the 1950s. Each letter was on a little rubber block, and you arranged them in slots to form words. The trouble was, they pinged off all over the place and ended up in the vacuum cleaner.

MOVABLE TYPE

With movable type, printing became easier. The printer Bi Sheng made Chinese characters from porcelain (a type of baked clay) around 1045. His type enabled thousands of copies to be printed.

The printer coats a metal plate with wax, then arranges porcelain characters on the wax to form words.

He warms the plate to soften the wax, then lays a flat board on the characters and presses them into the wax.

After inking the characters, he lays a sheet of paper over them and presses it to transfer the ink. Then he peels the paper off.

Yay! Only 1,285 pages still to print...

PRINTING PRESS

Printing with movable type became popular in Europe after Johannes Gutenberg introduced it to Germany in the 1440s. He also designed the first printing press. His early work for the church included printing the Bible. It took about half a day to arrange the letters for each page—and there were 1,286 pages! All told, it took his workers about three years to print 180 copies. But it was easier than writing the Bible out by hand.

SENDING OUT SIGNALS

The next time you text someone, spare a thought for your ancestors from before the computer age. Casually "chatting" involved things like smoke, mirrors, lights, and arm signals. But the rise of electric power in the 18th century brought a wave of new inventions based on the telegraph. At last they could send messages instantly over long distances simply by pressing keys.

> It says your home is on fire.

SMOKE SIGNALS

As soon as humans learned to control fire, they could control smoke by placing damp grass on a fire. Ancient Chinese and Greeks, as well as Native Americans, used smoke signals, often to warn others of danger.

Mechanical arms signaled using a special code with 196 combinations.

SEMAPHORE

Have you ever waved your arms to attract help? Frenchman Claude Chappe put this old trick to use when he invented a semaphore system in 1792. As each station received a signal, it passed it on to the next. Chappe's network of stations eventually spanned all of France.

> Bad signal today...

HELIOGRAPH

A mirror reflecting sunlight makes an excellent signaling device. German surveyors used this idea in the 1820s. About 1869, Henry Mance, a British official, invented the Mance heliograph, a sun-signaling instrument with a range of 35 miles (56 km).

FAX MACHINE

Alexander Bain was a canny Scotsman who invented the electric clock and also laid telegraph lines along the Edinburgh–Glasgow railway. In the 1840s, he devised one of the first faxes: machines that "telephone" exact copies of text and pictures to people. Few people use the fax with email available.

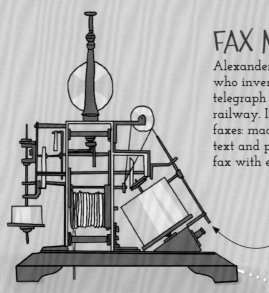

Some of the moving parts for Bain's fax machine came from his clock designs.

TELEGRAPH

The first really practical telegraph was invented in 1837 by William Cooke and Charles Wheatstone for use on the new railways that were snaking across Britain. It used five wires that sent signals to five magnetic needles, which then pointed to letters. Though easy to use, it was expensive, so they came up with a single-wire telegraph in 1845.

Letter

Needle

Electrical connectors

Dit... dit... dit-dit-dit... dah... this is driving me dotty.

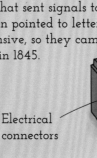

MORSE CODE

Morse code is named after American Samuel Morse, but others—Joseph Henry and Alfred Vail—helped with his 1836 invention. You used the electrical tapper to send a code of short signals (dots, or "dits") and long (dashes, or "dahs"), and the person at the other end decoded it to read the message.

RADIO

Radio, TV, computer, mobile phone, walkie-talkie–all of these communication tools use radio waves. Radio waves are similar to light waves but invisible, though just as fast. Once radio waves were understood, the race was on to invent new ways of communicating.

Electricity plus magnetism make...

RADIO WAVES

The discovery of radio waves began with Scotsman James Clerk Maxwell (*left*). In 1864, he suggested that magnetism and electricity working together could create invisible waves.

One full wave (from one crest to the next) is called a cycle. The length of one cycle is the wavelength.

...radio waves! Now we've got you!

In 1885, German scientist Heinrich Hertz (*right*) tested Maxwell's theory using a spark gap as an antenna. When a spark jumped the gap, it showed it had picked up radio waves. The cycle (waves per second) was named a hertz (Hz), in Heinrich's honor.

So who invented radio? We've lined up some suspects...

TESLA

Serbian **Nikola Tesla** worked in the United States for Thomas Edison, then on his own. He invented giant Tesla coils to send and receive radio waves. In 1892, he designed a radio, but his lab burnt down before he could test it. So Marconi is credited as the inventor of radio.

MARCONI

From 1894-1897, a young Italian, **Guglielmo Marconi**, used transmitters ("senders") and receivers ("getters") to send radio signals over steadily greater distances. He went to Britain and demonstrated his kit by transmitting across the Bristol Channel. In 1901, he sent a message over the Atlantic.

TRANSISTOR

The bulky vacuum tube was replaced in 1947 by the transistor. The first transistor, designed at Bell Labs in the US, looked like a tangle of burnt spaghetti, and it was big! Modern transistors are so tiny you can fit millions into 1 sq in (6.45 sq cm) of circuitboard.

The first transistor radios of the 1950s were portable—handy for annoying people.

An early radio set—the vacuum tubes made it very warm!

VACUUM TUBE

The vacuum tube, invented by Englishman John Fleming in 1904 and improved on by American Lee de Forest in 1907, allowed for big changes in current. It was used in radio, TV, and, from the 1940s, the first computers.

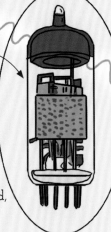

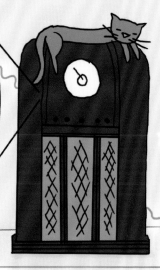

J C BOSE

Jagadish Chandra Bose of India was an all-round genius who also wrote sci-fi novels. His experiments with new equipment in the 1890s helped other radio pioneers (like Marconi), but he wasn't interested in making a system of communication.

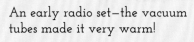

STUBBLEFIELD

Nathan Stubblefield, an American farmer, invented a kind of wireless broadcasting system in the 1880s-1890s. In 1902, he demonstrated it by sending a message "from Santa Claus" to some schoolkids in a field. But it wasn't true radio. It used magnetic induction.

TELEPHONE

Scottish-born Alexander Graham Bell usually gets the credit for inventing the first workable telephone in 1876, but over the next few years nearly 600 people challenged him with inventions of their own. The reason was money: if you could file a patent for one of the world's most useful inventions, you could make a lot of cash! And of course, people have done that, all the way up to Apple with its iPhone. Here are some of the highlights.

THE TRUTH...

Antonio Meucci, an Italian-American, invented a practical telephone before Bell, but his 1871 patent was unclearly worded, and Bell outsmarted him. Although Meucci died penniless in 1889, honor was restored 113 years later when the US Congress said that Bell had stolen his ideas.

ANOTHER VOICE

Johann Reis, a German schoolteacher, invented a telephone in 1861. It wasn't very good, but it worked, and Reis used an odd message to test it (*left*). He even came up with the name *telephon*, which means "far voice."

CAR PHONE

Early phones were, of course, connected to the wall by electric cable (and many still are). The first mobile phones came much later. This MTA model, made in 1956 by Swedish company Ericcson, was one of the first car phones—but you needed a big car!

SMARTPHONE

The first smartphone? Hmm, well. The Simon Personal Assistant, launched by IBM in 1994, enabled you to send emails and texts or check your calendar . . . but the battery only lasted about an hour!

IPHONE

The iPhone arrived in 2007 and was the brainchild of Steve Jobs (1955-2011), co-founder of Apple. Many Apple workers helped invent it. One was John Casey, who created the Telipod, from the iPod and a telephone, in 2000. This later became the iPhone.

VIDEOPHONE

In the mid-1960s, the Bell Company launched this Picturephone for making video calls, but it wasn't very successful. These days, we have apps such as Skype, invented in 2003 by Scandinavians Niklas Zennström and Janus Friis.

I can seeeeeee youuuu.

MOBILE NETWORKS

Mobile phones use mobile networks—ground stations that provide a connection. Some phones connect instead through the communications satellites orbiting Earth. The first satellite phone call was made on July 10th, 1962 using the newly launched Telstar 1 satellite.

Early Bird (1965) was one of the first communications satellites (comsats).

MOBILE PHONE

The first practical mobile phone was this Motorola DynaTAC of 1973. Martin Cooper at Motorola famously phoned Joel Engel at Bell Labs to tell him they'd beaten Bell to an invention.

CODE

Several communication methods use codes—the semaphore, the heliograph, and the Morse tapper used code to make their flags, flashes, and dit-dahs readable. But codes can also provide secrecy. Since ancient times, we've used code to keep messages out of enemy hands, and cracking important codes has helped countries win wars.

HIDDEN MESSAGE

Demaratus, a Greek living in Persia in 480 BCE, wanted to warn the Greeks that the Persians were building an army. So he took a wax notebook, scraped off the wax, and wrote his message on the wood base. Then he rewaxed it. This was smuggled to the Greeks, who scraped off the wax to find the message. Not really code, but still clever.

MESSAGE STICK

The people of Sparta, an ancient Greek city-state, wrote messages on strips of animal hide. They spaced the letters widely. When the recipient wrapped the strip around a wooden pole of the correct size, the letters lined up to reveal the message. You can do this code trick with a strip of paper around a pencil or a broom-handle.

HOBO CODE

Travelers in olden times used their own secret code. Wandering from town to town, they'd scratch marks on walls or gates to tell other travelers about friendly (or unfriendly) householders, a dangerous dog, easy pickings, and so on. Their sign language is sometimes known as "hobo code."

♭ = owner is in   Ⓧ = good place for a handout   ⊕ = hit the road

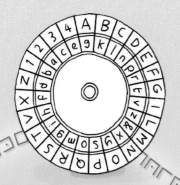

CIPHER DISK

This cipher disk was invented by Italian Leone Alberti in the 1460s. It has two discs of different sizes, each with an alphabet, and the two sets of letters can be lined up. The outer ring, or plaintext, is used to set messages into ciphertext (the inner ring). Decoding depends on knowing which two letters need to be lined up.

THE GREAT CIPHER

Codes used seriously—in war, for instance—can be very hard to break. In 1626 in France, Antoine Rossignol and his son invented a code in which each French syllable was represented by two or three numbers. Their code was known as The Great Cipher. It was so strong, no one cracked it until 1893!

Where are the French hiding?

Um... 34 - 561 - 192, Sir...

WE'RE ON A ROLL!

GUIDANCE SYSTEM

In the US, actress Hedy Lamarr and composer George Antheil invented a guidance system for torpedoes in World War II. It used a piano roll (from self-playing pianos) to create unbreakable codes. It was not used at the time, but it later led on to Wi-Fi and Bluetooth.

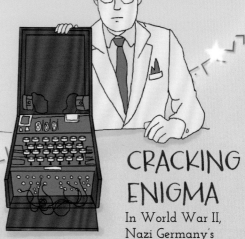

CRACKING ENIGMA

In World War II, Nazi Germany's secret messages were coded using a machine called Enigma, invented by Arthur Scherbius in 1918. The Poles were the first to crack the Enigma codes, and they taught their methods to the British, French, and Americans. This helped the Allies to win the war.

TV AND VIDEO

In TV's early days, to send an image you had to chop it up into bits, transmit the bits to a receiver, and then rearrange the image from the bits. The first efforts were mechanical—with moving parts—and the picture was fuzzy. It wasn't until better radio technology led to electronic broadcasting that crystal-clear pictures appeared on our screens.

NIPKOW DISK

Chopping up images began with an 1884 invention by German Paul Nipkow. The Nipkow disk was a spinning circle with a spiral of holes. It projected images onto a photo-electric sensor, which turned them into light/dark "messages." A second Nipkow disk unscrambled the messages to recreate the image.

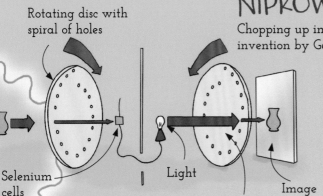

Rotating disc with spiral of holes

Selenium cells

Light

Image

Second disc rotating at the same speed

JOHN LOGIE BAIRD

The father of TV was arguably Scotsman John Logie Baird. He was so poor, he built his early equipment from junk. In 1928, he made the first transatlantic TV broadcast from London to New York. The next year, he began broadcasting for the new BBC television service.

JENKINS TV

In America, C. Francis Jenkins designed a Nipkow-style TV in 1923 and launched the US's first TV station in 1928. Francis also invented the waxed paper carton (for juice or milk) and an aircraft catapult.

THIS is entertainment!

Baird's first home-built TV scanner included some Nipkow disks, an old hatbox, darning needles, bike lights, and plenty of glue.

CATHODE RAY TUBE

Old TV sets—the fat, heavy ones—contained a cathode ray tube or CRT. Inside this, a beam of electrons shone at a phosphorescent (glowing) surface—the screen—to make the image. German scientist Karl Braun invented the first CRT in 1897, and Russian-born Vladimir Zworykin improved on it in the 1920s (example pictured). With the invention of the CRT, television had become electronic.

FLASH-MATIC

The world's first TV remote control was the Zenith Lazy-Bones of 1950. A wire connected it to the set. Much more space-age was Zenith's Flash-Matic of 1955, which shone a "magic light" at your TV to change the channel or volume. (Unless, of course, your dog was sitting in the way.)

Umm, Flash, geddout the way!

I can't see a thing, Bing!

VIDEO CASSETTE RECORDER

Before the invention of the DVD in 1995, the video cassette recorder (VCR) was used to record and play back programs. American singer Bing Crosby wanted to record his shows, so he helped the Ampex company develop the first VCR, the VR-1000, in the 1950s. It was as big as a gas cooking range!

COMPUTERS

The computer is perhaps the single most important invention of our time. The first computers, invented less than a century ago, were like dinosaurs–big body, small brain–but not so today. A single modern smartphone is millions of times more powerful than all of NASA's computers from 1969. (And they managed to put men on the Moon!)

WEAVING ORIGINS

The idea for the computer program came from the French weaving industry over 250 years ago. To weave a pattern on a Jacquard loom, you fit it with a chain of cards, each punched with a set of holes. The patterns of holes told the machine which threads to pick.

MECHANICAL COMPUTERS

Englishman Charles Babbage (1791-1871) designed the first mechanical computers: the Difference and the Analytical engines. They were huge, with thousands of moving parts for doing tough math. But he was never able to complete their construction.

COMPUTER WHIZZES

The first computer programmer was Ada Lovelace (*below*), daughter of famous poet Lord Byron. She worked for Charles Babbage. Grace Hopper (1906-1992) a rear-admiral in the US Navy, wrote computer code, including the COBOL language. It's said she also invented the term *computer bug* when a moth fell into her equipment.

DATA

The US Census Bureau collected information on American citizens, such as birth and marriage dates. To help sort the data, Herman Hollerith, a Bureau worker, invented a series of tabulating machines from the 1890s onwards. These used hole-punched cards to hold the data.

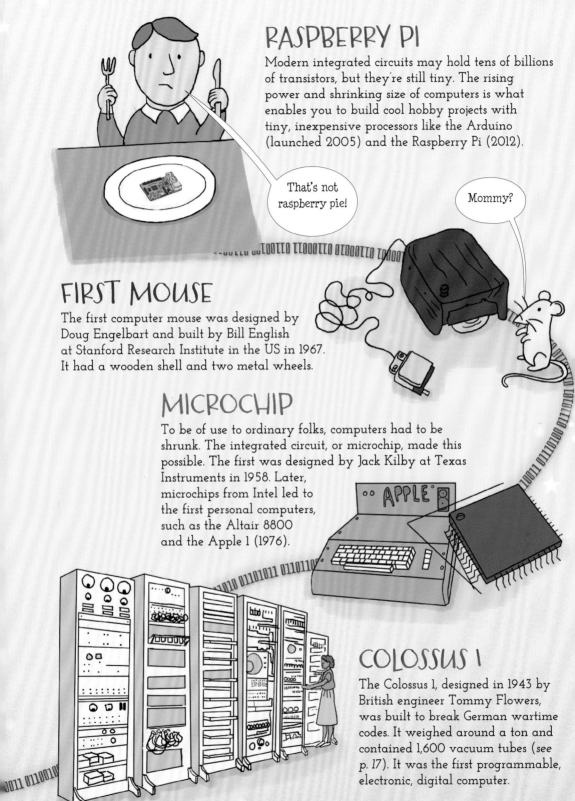

RASPBERRY PI

Modern integrated circuits may hold tens of billions of transistors, but they're still tiny. The rising power and shrinking size of computers is what enables you to build cool hobby projects with tiny, inexpensive processors like the Arduino (launched 2005) and the Raspberry Pi (2012).

That's not raspberry pie!

Mommy?

FIRST MOUSE

The first computer mouse was designed by Doug Engelbart and built by Bill English at Stanford Research Institute in the US in 1967. It had a wooden shell and two metal wheels.

MICROCHIP

To be of use to ordinary folks, computers had to be shrunk. The integrated circuit, or microchip, made this possible. The first was designed by Jack Kilby at Texas Instruments in 1958. Later, microchips from Intel led to the first personal computers, such as the Altair 8800 and the Apple 1 (1976).

COLOSSUS 1

The Colossus 1, designed in 1943 by British engineer Tommy Flowers, was built to break German wartime codes. It weighed around a ton and contained 1,600 vacuum tubes (*see p. 17*). It was the first programmable, electronic, digital computer.

THE INTERNET

Just a few decades ago, the Internet was a bit like a club, open only to certain groups, such as scientists and government departments. These days, going online is as easy as picking up the phone. Every day, more than a billion people use Facebook. Every minute, over 300 hours of video are uploaded to YouTube. But where did it all begin?

ARPANET

The first version of the Internet was ARPANET. The network was set up in 1969 just for DARPA: the Defense Advanced Research Projects Agency. This US government department of inventors wanted to share ideas between chosen groups. One way of sharing was by email, which was invented @ ARPANET by Ray Tomlinson in 1972.

PACKET-SWITCHING

The Internet communicates by packet-switching. This is a way of sending little electronic "packets" of data along shared pathways. It was created in the 1960s by Leonard Kleinrock and Paul Baran in the US, and Donald Davies in the UK. In 1973, Vint Cerf and Bob Kahn in the US wrote TCP: the rules for packet-switching. That year, ARPANET became the Internet and went international.

WORLD WIDE WEB

The World Wide Web (WWW) is all the information on the Internet. It was created by English computer scientist Tim Berners-Lee. In the 1980s, Tim worked with CERN, a European nuclear research organization. He invented HTML (Hyper Text Markup Language), and CERN began using it on what was to be the world's first web page.

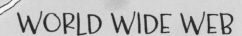

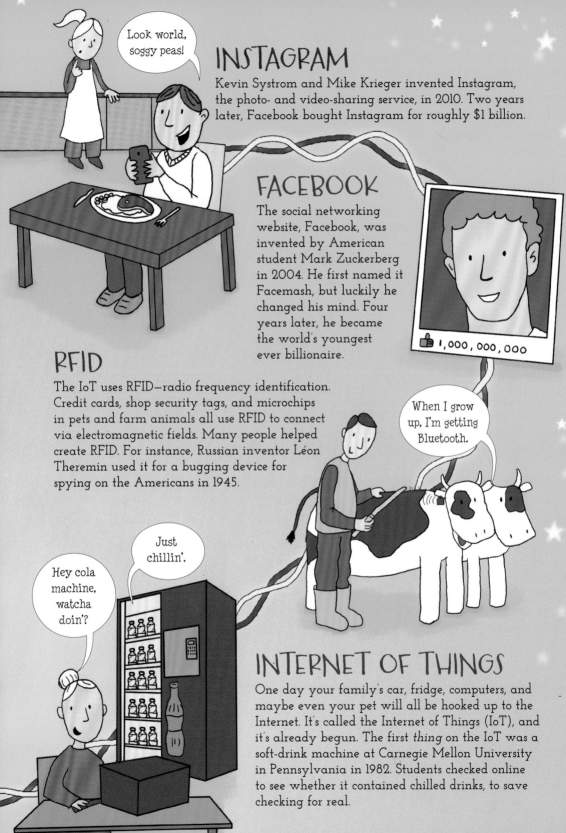

INSTAGRAM

Kevin Systrom and Mike Krieger invented Instagram, the photo- and video-sharing service, in 2010. Two years later, Facebook bought Instagram for roughly $1 billion.

FACEBOOK

The social networking website, Facebook, was invented by American student Mark Zuckerberg in 2004. He first named it Facemash, but luckily he changed his mind. Four years later, he became the world's youngest ever billionaire.

RFID

The IoT uses RFID—radio frequency identification. Credit cards, shop security tags, and microchips in pets and farm animals all use RFID to connect via electromagnetic fields. Many people helped create RFID. For instance, Russian inventor Léon Theremin used it for a bugging device for spying on the Americans in 1945.

INTERNET OF THINGS

One day your family's car, fridge, computers, and maybe even your pet will all be hooked up to the Internet. It's called the Internet of Things (IoT), and it's already begun. The first *thing* on the IoT was a soft-drink machine at Carnegie Mellon University in Pennsylvania in 1982. Students checked online to see whether it contained chilled drinks, to save checking for real.

27

WACKY INVENTIONS

The brilliant English scientist Stephen Hawking once said, "Mankind's greatest achievements have come about by talking, and its greatest failures by not talking." So true—but talking isn't always easy. Just look at some of these crazy communication inventions.

It's great-uncle Bill

DIAL-A-GHOST

It is reported that in 1920, Thomas Edison, one of America's most famous inventors, proposed making a *spirit telephone* for talking to ghosts. This story is quite probably made up—but it's a good one.

BAIRD IDEAS...

John Logie Baird came up with good inventions—like the television and thermal socks—but some bad ones too. For example:

• Glass razorblades. His idea was to make a razor that wouldn't go rusty. Trouble was, it just shattered. Ouch!

• Artificial diamonds. Diamonds are a form of carbon. Graphite (pencil lead) is also a form of carbon. Diamonds are made naturally underground, by high pressure and temperature. Baird figured he could make them by heating graphite. But all he made was trouble when his experiment cut the power to the city of Glasgow, leaving everyone in the dark.

What happened to the lights!?

HOT TENNIS BALLS

American inventor Marvin Middlemark made millions from his Rabbit Ears TV antenna of 1953. He was less successful with a water-powered potato peeler and a plan to rejuvenate tennis balls by microwaving them.

BOW-LINGUAL

Want to chat to your dog? In 2002, a Japanese team invented a machine that listens to your dog's barking and translates it into an emotion (such as happy or sad), which is shown on a screen. Different versions have been made for different doggy dialects around the world.

PAWSENSE

You know when the cat walks across the keyboard, turning your homework into gobbledy-gook? This piece of computer software could save you. Whenever it detects cat-like typing, it sounds an alarm (which annoys the cat and drives it away) and "locks down" the keyboard.

CAMPILLO LOONYGRAPH

Some early versions of the telegraph—and there were many of them—were a bit crazy. In 1795 Spanish scientist Francisco Salva Campillo suggested connecting a group of people to electric wires. Each person stood for a different letter or number. Messages coming down the wires would shock each person, who would cry out their letter, spelling out the message. Eek!

29

DAFT PREDICTIONS

It's easy to look back through history and laugh at some of the crazy things people believed or said. At the time, of course, they didn't know any better, so it's not really their fault. But some of these quotes might still make you chuckle!

THE FUTURE OF MOVIES

"The cinema is little more than a fad."
—Charlie Chaplin, actor and film director, 1916

THE FUTURE OF MOVIE SOUND

"Who . . . wants to hear actors talk?"
—Harry Warner, president of the Warner Bros movie company, 1925

(These days, of course, 99.999999999 percent of movies are "talkies.")

THE FUTURE OF THE TELEPHONE

"The Americans have need of the telephone, but we do not. We have plenty of messenger boys."
—William Preece, chief engineer at the British Post Office, 1879

(These days, 93 percent of adults own a mobile phone.)

THE FUTURE OF WAR

"The coming of the wireless era will make war impossible, because it will make war ridiculous."
—Guglielmo Marconi, radio pioneer, 1912

(It may be ridiculous, but sadly, wireless has only helped people wage war.)

THE FUTURE OF COMPUTERS

"There is a world market for maybe five computers."
—Thomas Watson, head of computer company IBM, 1943

(These days there are more than two billion personal computers around the world.)

"Computers of the future may weigh no more than 1.5 tons."
—Popular Mechanics magazine, 1949

(Well, at least they were right about that—thank goodness!)

THE FUTURE OF THE INTERNET

"I predict the Internet will soon go spectacularly supernova and in 1996 catastrophically collapse."
—Robert Metcalfe, founder of computer network company 3Com, 1995.

(Bob promised to eat his words if he was wrong—which, as we now know, he was! Two years later, he used a kitchen blender to liquefy a printout of his prediction and then drank it.)

INDEX

The Author

British-born Matt Turner graduated from Loughborough College of Art in the 1980s, since which he has worked as a picture researcher, editor, and writer. He has authored books on diverse topics including natural history, earth sciences, and railways, as well as hundreds of articles for encyclopedias and partworks, covering everything from elephants to abstract art. He and his family currently live near Auckland, Aotearoa/New Zealand, where he volunteers for the local Coastguard unit and dabbles in art and craft.

The Illustrator

Sarah Conner lives in the lovely English countryside, in a cute cottage with her dogs and a cat. She spends her days sketching and doodling the world around her. She has always been inspired by nature and it influences much of her work. Sarah formerly used pens and paint for her illustration, but in recent years, she has transferred her styles to the computer as it better suits the current industry. However, she still likes to get her watercolors out from time to time and paint the flowers in her garden!